LE CORDON BLEU
HOME COLLECTION
·MUFFINS·

MURDOCH BOOKS®
Sydney • London • Vancouver • New York

contents

4
Apple muffins

6
Lemon muffins

8
Banana and ginger muffins

10
Blueberry muffins

12
White chocolate muffins

14
Raisin muffins

16
English muffins

18
Pear and pecan muffins

20
Apricot muffins

22
Mocha muffins

24
Chocolate and walnut muffins

26
Orange and poppy seed muffins

28
Prune muffins

30
American chocolate-chip muffins

32
Bran muffins

34
Fruit and nut muffins

36
Chocolate and orange muffins

38
Date and walnut muffins

40
Muesli muffins

42
Passion fruit and yoghurt muffins

44
Raspberry streusel muffins

46
Pumpkin muffins

48
Corn muffins

50
Seeded cheese muffins

52
Cheese and herb muffins

54
Bacon muffins

56
Olive, rosemary and Parmesan muffins

58
Red capsicum and feta muffins

60
Ham and cheese muffins

62
Chef's techniques

recipe ratings ❋ *easy* ❋❋ *a little more care needed* ❋❋❋ *more care needed*

Apple muffins

Moist and sweet, enhanced with the flavour of spices, these muffins are good enough to eat at any time of day, whether breakfast, brunch or afternoon tea.

*Preparation time **25 minutes***
*Total cooking time **30 minutes***
Makes 6 large muffins

225 g (7¹/4 oz) self-raising flour
150 g (5 oz) plain flour
1¹/2 teaspoons baking powder
2 teaspoons ground cinnamon
1 teaspoon ground nutmeg
3 tablespoons caster sugar
155 g (5 oz) unsalted butter
3 tablespoons honey
2 eggs
170 ml (5¹/2 fl oz) milk
3 green apples, peeled and
  cut into small chunks
1 teaspoon ground cinnamon, extra
2 tablespoons caster sugar, extra

1 Preheat the oven to moderately hot 200°C (400°F/ Gas 6). Grease a 6-hole (250 ml/8 fl oz capacity) muffin tin with melted butter or oil. Sift the flours, baking powder, cinnamon, nutmeg and sugar into a large bowl, and make a well in the centre.

2 Melt the butter and honey in a small saucepan over low heat, stirring continuously until smooth. Remove from the heat. Whisk the eggs and milk in a small jug.

3 Add the butter mixture, egg mixture and apple chunks to the well in the dry ingredients all at once. Using a metal spoon, stir until just combined. Do not overmix—the mixture should be lumpy.

4 Spoon the mixture into the muffin tin, filling each hole about three-quarters full. Sprinkle with the combined extra cinnamon and sugar. Bake for 20–25 minutes, or until a skewer comes out clean when inserted into the centre of a muffin. Leave the muffins in the tin for 10 minutes before lifting out onto a wire rack to cool.

Lemon muffins

The soft cream cheese icing generously spread onto these tangy lemon muffins makes them quite irresistible. When using lemon rind as a flavouring, it is essential to grate only the yellow skin of the lemon and not the white pith, which will be bitter.

Preparation time **20 minutes**
Total cooking time **12 minutes**
Makes 8 medium muffins

300 g (10 oz) self-raising flour
1/4 teaspoon baking powder
125 g (4 oz) caster sugar
2 tablespoons grated lemon rind
185 ml (6 fl oz) buttermilk
1 teaspoon vanilla extract or essence
2 eggs, lightly beaten
110 g (3 3/4 oz) unsalted butter, melted

ICING
20 g (3/4 oz) unsalted butter, softened
100 g (3 1/4 oz) cream cheese
2 tablespoons icing sugar
1 tablespoon lemon juice

shreds of lemon rind, to decorate

1 Preheat the oven to moderately hot 200°C (400°F/ Gas 6). Grease a 12-hole (125 ml/4 fl oz capacity) muffin tin with melted butter or oil. Sift the flour, baking powder and sugar into a large mixing bowl, stir in the lemon rind and make a well in the centre.

2 Mix the buttermilk, vanilla and eggs together in a small jug.

3 Add the butter and the egg mixture to the well in the dry ingredients. Using a metal spoon, stir until the mixture is just combined. Do not overmix—the mixture should be lumpy.

4 Spoon the mixture into eight holes of the muffin tin, filling each hole about three-quarters full. Bake for 10–12 minutes, or until a skewer comes out clean when inserted into the centre of a muffin. Leave in the tin for 5 minutes before lifting out onto a wire rack to cool.

5 To make the icing, beat the butter and cream cheese with electric beaters until well mixed. Add the icing sugar and lemon juice, and beat until thick and creamy. Spread the icing over the muffins when they are completely cold. Decorate with shreds of lemon rind.

Banana and ginger muffins

A subtle combination of banana and ginger, enhanced with the golden
nectar of honey, giving a lovely rich muffin.

Preparation time **20 minutes**
Total cooking time **25 minutes**
Makes 12 medium muffins

300 g (10 oz) self-raising flour
1 teaspoon ground ginger
115 g (3³/4 oz) soft brown sugar
75 g (2¹/2 oz) glacé ginger, finely chopped
60 g (2 oz) unsalted butter
2 tablespoons honey
125 ml (4 fl oz) milk
2 eggs
240 g (7¹/2 oz) banana, mashed (see Chef's tip)

TOPPING
125 g (4 oz) cream cheese, softened
2 tablespoons icing sugar
2 teaspoons finely grated lemon rind

glacé ginger, to decorate

1 Preheat the oven to hot 210°C (415°F/Gas 6–7). Brush a 12-hole (125 ml/4 fl oz capacity) muffin tin with melted butter or oil. Sift the flour and ground ginger together into a large mixing bowl. Stir in the brown sugar and glacé ginger, and make a well in the centre of the mixture.

2 Place the butter and honey in a small pan and stir over low heat until melted. Remove from the heat. Whisk the milk and eggs together in a jug.

3 Add the butter mixture, egg mixture and the banana to the well in the dry ingredients. Stir with a metal spoon until just combined. Do not overmix—the mixture should be lumpy. Spoon the mixture into the muffin tin, filling each hole about three-quarters full. Bake for 20 minutes, or until a skewer comes out clean when inserted into the centre of a muffin. Leave the muffins in the tin for 5 minutes, then lift out onto a wire rack to cool completely before spreading with the topping.

4 To make the topping, beat the cream cheese, icing sugar and grated lemon rind together until light and creamy. Spread onto the muffins and decorate with thin slices of glacé ginger.

Chef's tip You will need two medium ripe bananas for this recipe.

Blueberry muffins

These classic muffins may be made with either fresh or frozen blueberries, and are particularly good served warm for breakfast or morning tea. Try substituting raspberries or blackberries or a combination of these, gently folding them in to keep them whole.

Preparation time **15 minutes**
Total cooking time **30 minutes**
Makes 6 large muffins

375 g (12 oz) self-raising flour
75 g (2¹/₂ oz) plain flour
115 g (3³/₄ oz) soft brown sugar
150 g (5 oz) fresh or frozen blueberries (see Chef's tip)
2 eggs
250 ml (8 fl oz) milk
1 teaspoon vanilla extract or essence
125 g (4 oz) unsalted butter, melted
icing sugar, to dust

1 Preheat the oven to hot 210°C (415°F/Gas 6–7). Brush a 6-hole (250 ml/8 fl oz capacity) muffin tin with melted butter or oil. Sift the flours into a large mixing bowl, stir in the sugar and blueberries, and make a well in the centre.

2 Whisk the eggs, milk and vanilla together in a jug, and add to the well in the dry ingredients. Add the butter, and stir with a metal spoon until just combined. Do not overmix—the mixture should be lumpy.

3 Spoon the mixture into the muffin tin, filling each hole about three-quarters full. Bake for 30 minutes, or until a skewer comes out clean when inserted into the centre of a muffin. Leave the the muffins in the tin for 5 minutes before lifting out onto a wire rack to cool. Dust generously with sifted icing sugar before serving.

Chef's tip If using frozen blueberries, use them straight from the freezer. Do not allow them to thaw, or they will discolour the muffin mixture.

White chocolate muffins

The crunchy topping of flaked almonds provides a pleasant contrast to the soft white chocolate and lemon muffin.

Preparation time **20 minutes**
Total cooking time **25 minutes**
Makes 6 large muffins

375 g (12 oz) self-raising flour
125 g (4 oz) caster sugar
200 g (6¹/2 oz) white chocolate, chopped
2 eggs
375 ml (12 fl oz) milk
2 teaspoons finely grated lemon rind
160 g (5¹/4 oz) unsalted butter, melted
45 g (1¹/2 oz) flaked almonds

1 Preheat the oven to hot 210°C (415°F/Gas 6–7). Brush a 6-hole (250 ml/8 fl oz capacity) muffin tin with melted butter or oil. Sift the flour into a large mixing bowl, stir in the sugar and chocolate, and make a well in the centre.

2 Whisk the eggs, milk and lemon rind together in a jug, and pour into the well in the dry ingredients. Add the butter, and stir with a metal spoon until the mixture is just combined. Do not overmix—the mixture should be lumpy.

3 Spoon the mixture into the muffin tin, filling each hole to about three-quarters full. Sprinkle flaked almonds on top of the mixture and gently press them on. Bake for 25 minutes, or until a skewer comes out clean when inserted into the centre of a muffin. Leave the muffins in the tin for 5 minutes before lifting out onto a wire rack to cool.

Raisin muffins

*Serve these spicy raisin muffins warm with lightly sweetened whipped butter
as an alternative to plain butter. Try using sultanas or dates as a substitute for raisins.*

*Preparation time **25 minutes***
*Total cooking time **20 minutes***
Makes 12 medium muffins

150 g (5 oz) self-raising flour
155 g (5 oz) wholemeal self-raising flour
1/2 teaspoon ground ginger
1/2 teaspoon mixed spice
115 g (3³/4 oz) soft brown sugar
260 g (8¹/2 oz) raisins
2 eggs
185 ml (6 fl oz) milk
125 g (4 oz) unsalted butter, melted
icing sugar, to dust

WHIPPED BUTTER
60 g (2 oz) unsalted butter, softened
1/4 teaspoon vanilla extract or essence
1 tablespoon icing sugar

1 Preheat the oven to hot 210°C (415°F/Gas 6–7).
Brush a 12-hole (125 ml/4 fl oz capacity) muffin tin
with melted butter or oil. Sift the flours, ginger and
spice into a large mixing bowl, returning the husks from
the sifter to the bowl. Stir in the sugar and raisins, and
make a well in the centre.

2 Whisk the eggs and milk together in a jug and add to
the well in the dry ingredients along with the melted
butter. Using a metal spoon, stir until just combined. Do
not overmix—the mixture should be lumpy.

3 Spoon the mixture into the muffin tin, filling each
hole about three-quarters full. Bake for 20 minutes, or
until a skewer comes out clean when inserted into the
centre of a muffin. Leave the muffins in the tin for
5 minutes before lifting out onto a wire rack to cool.

4 To make the whipped butter, beat the butter with a
wooden spoon in a small bowl until it is light and
creamy. Beat in the vanilla and the sifted icing sugar.
Dust the muffins with sifted icing sugar before serving
with the whipped butter.

English muffins

English muffins were originally lightly split around the edges using a fork, then toasted on both sides, pulled open and spread thickly with butter.

Preparation time **30 minutes**
    + 1 hour 20 minutes proving
Total cooking time **15 minutes**
Makes 12

10 g (1/4 oz) fresh yeast or 2 teaspoons dried yeast
400 g (12 3/4 oz) strong or plain flour
1 1/2 teaspoons salt
1 teaspoon caster sugar
1 teaspoon softened unsalted butter

1 Gently heat 225 ml (7 1/4 fl oz) water in a small pan until it feels warm, not hot, to the touch. Remove from the heat and stir in the yeast until it is dissolved.

2 Sift the flour, salt and caster sugar into a large bowl, make a well in the centre and pour in the yeast mixture. Melt the butter (again, it should not be too hot) and pour it into the well. Using your hand with fingers slightly spread apart, gradually bring the flour into the liquid and mix well. Turn the dough out onto a floured work surface and knead for 2–3 minutes, or until smooth.

3 Place the dough in a clean bowl that has been sprinkled with a little flour. Cover with plastic wrap and leave in a warm place for about 1 hour, or until doubled in size.

4 Sprinkle a baking tray with flour. Preheat the oven to hot 210°C (415°F/Gas 6–7). Turn the dough out onto a lightly floured work surface and knead until smooth. Roll the dough to about 1 cm (1/2 inch) thick and, using a 7 cm (2 3/4 inch) plain round cutter dipped in flour, cut out rounds and place them on the baking tray. Re-roll any leftover dough and repeat. Cover the tray with plastic wrap and leave in a warm place for 15–20 minutes, or until the muffins have risen slightly. Bake for 15 minutes, turning halfway through the cooking time. Remove from the tray and cool on a wire rack.

Chef's tip These muffins can also be cooked on top of the stove using a griddle or dry pan over low heat. Turn over as each side becomes lightly browned and is cooked through.

Pear and pecan muffins

*The soft cooked pear contributes to the lovely moist texture of these muffins
with the added crunch and flavour of chopped toasted pecans.*

*Preparation time **25 minutes***
*Total cooking time **30 minutes***
Makes 6 large muffins

300 g (10 oz) self-raising flour
150 g (5 oz) plain flour
1 teaspoon ground cinnamon
1/2 teaspoon ground nutmeg
115 g (3³/4 oz) soft brown sugar
400 g (12³/4 oz) pears, peeled, cored and finely
chopped
100 g (3¹/4 oz) pecans, toasted and chopped
(see Chef's tip)
2 eggs
375 ml (12 fl oz) milk
1 teaspoon vanilla extract or essence
125 g (4 oz) unsalted butter, melted

6 whole pecans, to decorate
icing sugar, to dust

1 Preheat the oven to hot 210°C (415°F/Gas 6–7). Brush a 6-hole (250 ml/8 fl oz capacity) muffin tin with melted butter or oil. Sift the flours, cinnamon and nutmeg into a large mixing bowl, and stir in the sugar, pear and pecans.

2 Whisk the eggs, milk and vanilla together in a jug and pour them into the well in the dry ingredients. Add the butter and stir with a metal spoon until the mixture is just combined. Do not overmix—the mixture should be lumpy.

3 Spoon the mixture into the muffin tin, filling each hole about three-quarters full. Press a pecan onto the top of each muffin and bake for 30 minutes, or until a skewer comes out clean when inserted into the centre of a muffin. Leave in the tin for 5 minutes before lifting out onto a wire rack to cool. Dust with sifted icing sugar before serving.

Chef's tip To toast the nuts, spread them on a baking tray and bake in a moderate 180°C (350°F/Gas 4) oven for 5–7 minutes, or until lightly browned.

Apricot muffins

These fruity muffins, made with dried apricots and wholemeal flour, are best eaten on the day they are made. Use other fruits such as dried peaches or figs as an alternative, or mixed spice in place of the cinnamon.

Preparation time **25 minutes**
Total cooking time **25 minutes**
Makes 12 medium muffins

180 g (5³/4 oz) dried apricots, chopped
125 ml (4 fl oz) orange juice
185 g (6 oz) plain flour
195 g (6¹/4 oz) wholemeal self-raising flour
1¹/2 teaspoons ground cinnamon
165 g (5¹/2 oz) soft brown sugar
185 ml (6 fl oz) milk
1 egg
185 g (6 oz) unsalted butter, melted
icing sugar, to dust

1 Preheat the oven to hot 210°C (415°F/Gas 6–7). Brush a 12-hole (125 ml/4 fl oz capacity) muffin tin with melted butter or oil. Place the apricots in a small bowl. Warm the orange juice and pour it over the apricots, then leave to cool.

2 Sift the flours and cinnamon into a large mixing bowl, and return the husks to the bowl. Stir in the sugar, and make a well in the centre.

3 Whisk the milk and egg together in a jug and pour into the well in the dry ingredients with the butter, apricots and juice. Stir with a metal spoon until the mixture is just combined. Do not overmix—the mixture should be lumpy.

4 Spoon the mixture into the muffin tin, filling each hole about three-quarters full. Bake for 20 minutes, or until a skewer comes out clean when inserted into the centre of a muffin. Leave in the tin for 5 minutes before lifting out onto a wire rack to cool. Sprinkle the tops of the muffins lightly with sifted icing sugar before serving.

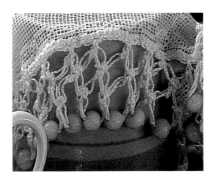

Mocha muffins

Mocha was originally the name of a strong Arabian coffee with a distinctive aroma, shipped from Yemen's port of Mocha. Today, mocha often refers to a hot chocolate- and coffee-flavoured drink or to the combination of these two flavours used in cakes, biscuits or, as in this case, muffins.

*Preparation time **20 minutes***
*Total cooking time **25 minutes***
Makes 12 medium muffins

375 ml (12 fl oz) milk
1 tablespoon instant coffee powder or granules
200 g (6¹/₂ oz) self-raising flour
200 g (6¹/₂ oz) plain flour
4 tablespoons cocoa powder
115 g (3³/₄ oz) soft brown sugar
2 eggs, lightly beaten
160 g (5¹/₄ oz) unsalted butter, melted
125 ml (4 fl oz) cream, whipped
drinking chocolate, to dust

1 Preheat the oven to hot 210°C (415°F/Gas 6–7). Brush a 12-hole (125 ml/4 fl oz capacity) muffin tin with melted butter or oil. Heat the milk in a small saucepan over medium heat, without boiling, and add the coffee powder or granules. Stir until dissolved, then set aside to cool.

2 Sift the flours and cocoa powder into a large mixing bowl, stir in the sugar and make a well in the centre. Add the milk mixture, the eggs and the butter to the well in the dry ingredients, and stir with a metal spoon until just combined. Do not overmix—the mixture should be lumpy.

3 Spoon the mixture into the muffin tin, filling each hole about three-quarters full. Bake for 20 minutes, or until a skewer comes out clean when inserted into the centre of a muffin. Leave the muffins in the tin for 5 minutes before lifting out onto a wire rack to cool completely before decorating.

4 Top each muffin with a spoonful of whipped cream, and dust with the sifted drinking chocolate.

Chocolate and walnut muffins

These rich dark chocolate muffins freeze very well—simply allow to cool completely and seal in airtight freezer containers or bags for up to a month. To serve, thaw the muffins at room temperature and reheat in a moderate oven if desired.

Preparation time **20 minutes**
Total cooking time **20 minutes**
Makes 12 medium muffins

265 g (8¹/2 oz) self-raising flour
4 tablespoons plain flour
¹/2 teaspoon baking powder
3 tablespoons cocoa powder
150 g (5 oz) unsalted butter
165 g (5¹/2 oz) soft brown sugar
170 ml (5¹/2 fl oz) milk
2 eggs
100 g (3¹/4 oz) walnuts,
  chopped
125 g (4 oz) dark chocolate,
  roughly chopped
icing sugar, to dust

1 Preheat the oven to moderately hot 200°C (400°F/ Gas 6). Grease a 12-hole (125 ml/4 fl oz capacity) muffin tin with melted butter or oil. Sift the flours, baking powder and cocoa into a large mixing bowl.

2 Stir the butter and sugar in a small saucepan over low heat until the butter is melted and the sugar has dissolved. Remove from the heat. Mix the milk and eggs together in a small jug.

3 Add the chopped walnuts and chocolate to the dry ingredients, and make a well in the centre. Pour the butter and egg mixtures into the well, and stir with a metal spoon until the mixture is just combined. Do not overmix—the mixture should be lumpy.

4 Spoon into the muffin tin, filling each hole about three-quarters full. Bake for 15–18 minutes, or until a skewer comes out clean when inserted into the centre of a muffin. Leave in the tin for 5 minutes before lifting out onto a wire rack to cool. Dust with sifted icing sugar.

Orange and poppy seed muffins

Countless poppy seeds are scattered liberally throughout these mufffins, filling them with a delightful flavour and delicate crunch.

*Preparation time **20 minutes***
*Total cooking time **20 minutes***
Makes 10 medium muffins

300 g (10 oz) self-raising flour
1/4 teaspoon baking powder
3 tablespoons caster sugar
2 tablespoons poppy seeds
1 1/2 tablespoons finely grated orange rind
100 g (3 1/4 oz) unsalted butter
105 g (3 1/2 oz) apricot jam
2 eggs
80 ml (2 3/4 fl oz) buttermilk
icing sugar, to dust

1 Preheat the oven to moderately hot 200°C (400°F/ Gas 6). Grease a 12-hole (125 ml/4 fl oz capacity) muffin tin with melted butter or oil. Sift the flour, baking powder and sugar into a large bowl. Stir in the poppy seeds and grated orange rind, and make a well in the centre.

2 Melt the butter and jam in a small saucepan over low heat, stirring until smooth. Remove from the heat. Mix the eggs and buttermilk together in a small jug.

3 Add the butter and egg mixtures to the well in the dry ingredients. Stir with a metal spoon until the mixture is just combined. Do not overmix—the mixture should be lumpy.

4 Spoon the mixture into ten holes of the muffin tin, filling each hole about three-quarters full. Bake for 12–15 minutes, or until a skewer comes out clean when inserted into the centre of a muffin. Leave the muffins in the tin for 5 minutes before carefully lifting out onto a wire rack to cool. Dust lightly with sifted icing sugar before serving.

Prune muffins

The combination of rich dark prunes and rolled oats makes this an excellent muffin for the health conscious. The crunchy sweet oat topping is optional, but is highly recommended for its added flavour and crunch.

Preparation time **25 minutes**
Total cooking time **20 minutes**
Makes 12 medium muffins

150 g (5 oz) self-raising flour
75 g (2¹/2 oz) plain flour
75 g (2¹/2 oz) wholemeal self-raising flour
115 g (3³/4 oz) soft brown sugar
50 g (1³/4 oz) rolled oats
110 g (3³/4 oz) pitted prunes, chopped
2 eggs
250 ml (8 fl oz) milk
100 g (3¹/4 oz) unsalted butter, melted

STREUSEL TOPPING
1 tablespoon plain flour
¹/2 teaspoon ground cinnamon
¹/4 teaspoon ground nutmeg
55 g (1³/4 oz) soft brown sugar

4 tablespoons rolled oats
20 g (³/4 oz) unsalted butter, melted

1 Preheat the oven to hot 210°C (415°F/Gas 6–7). Brush a 12-hole (125 ml/4 fl oz capacity) muffin tin with melted butter or oil. Sift the flours into a large mixing bowl, returning the husks to the bowl. Stir in the sugar, oats and prunes, and make a well in the centre.

2 Whisk together the eggs and milk, and pour into the well in the dry ingredients along with the butter. Stir with a metal spoon until just combined. Do not overmix—the mixture should be lumpy. Spoon the mixture into the muffin tin, filling each hole about three-quarters full.

3 To make the topping, place all the ingredients in a small bowl and mix well. Sprinkle over the tops of the unbaked muffins, and press gently. Bake for 20 minutes, or until a skewer comes out clean when inserted into the centre of a muffin. Leave the muffins in the tin for 5 minutes before lifting out onto a wire rack to cool.

American chocolate-chip muffins

If chocolate chips are not available to make these decadent chocolate muffins, simply use chopped dark chocolate.

Preparation time **15 minutes**
Total cooking time **30 minutes**
Makes 6 large muffins

225 g (7¹/4 oz) self-raising flour
75 g (2¹/2 oz) plain flour
4 tablespoons cocoa powder
115 g (3³/4 oz) soft brown sugar
265 g (8¹/2 oz) dark chocolate chips
2 eggs
375 ml (12 fl oz) buttermilk
90 g (3 oz) unsalted butter, melted
2 tablespoons dark chocolate chips, extra
icing sugar, to dust

1 Preheat the oven to hot 210°C (415°F/Gas 6–7). Brush a 6-hole (250 ml/8 fl oz capacity) muffin tin with melted butter or oil. Sift the flours and cocoa powder into a large mixing bowl, stir in the sugar and chocolate chips, and make a well in the centre.

2 Whisk the eggs and buttermilk together in a jug, and pour into the well in the dry ingredients along with the butter. Stir with a metal spoon until just combined. Do not overmix—the mixture should be lumpy.

3 Spoon the mixture into the muffin tin, filling each hole about three-quarters full. Sprinkle with the extra chocolate chips, pressing them on gently. Bake for 30 minutes, or until a skewer comes out clean when inserted into the centre of a muffin. Leave the muffins in the tin for 5 minutes before lifting out onto a wire rack to cool. Dust with sifted icing sugar before serving.

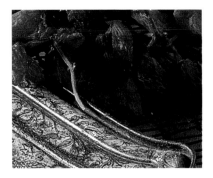

Bran muffins

High in fibre and sweetened only with honey, these healthy muffins make an excellent start to the day. They are best eaten warm with a little butter on the day they are made.

Preparation time **20 minutes**
Total cooking time **25 minutes**
Makes 12 medium muffins

225 g (7¹/4 oz) self-raising flour
75 g (2¹/2 oz) unprocessed bran
185 g (6 oz) sultanas
90 g (3 oz) unsalted butter
4 tablespoons honey
2 eggs
250 g (8 oz) plain yoghurt

1 Preheat the oven to hot 210°C (415°F/Gas 6–7). Line a 12-hole (125 ml/4 fl oz capacity) muffin tin with paper muffin cases. Sift the flour into a large mixing bowl, stir in the bran and sultanas, and make a well in the centre.

2 Place the butter and honey in a small pan, and stir over low heat until melted and well mixed. Remove from the heat. Whisk together the eggs and yoghurt, and pour into the well in the dry ingredients along with the butter and honey mixture. Stir with a metal spoon until just combined. Do not overmix—the mixture should be lumpy.

3 Spoon the mixture into the muffin tin, filling each hole about three-quarters full. Bake for 20 minutes, or until a skewer comes out clean when inserted into the centre of a muffin. Leave the muffins in the tin for 5 minutes before lifting out onto a wire rack to cool. Serve warm or cold with butter.

Chef's tip Paper muffin cases are available from some supermarkets or from speciality kitchen shops. If they are not available, brush the muffin tin with melted butter or oil before using.

Fruit and nut muffins

This recipe calls for dried mixed fruit, pecans and hazelnuts; however, one could use any single type of dried fruit with either walnuts or almonds, or a combination of nuts.

*Preparation time **20 minutes***
*Total cooking time **20 minutes***
Makes 12 medium muffins

225 g (7¼ oz) self-raising flour
55 g (1¾ oz) wholemeal plain flour
½ teaspoon baking powder
2 teaspoons mixed spice
½ teaspoon ground allspice
1 teaspoon ground ginger
150 g (5 oz) unsalted butter
55 g (1¾ oz) soft brown sugar
3 tablespoons treacle
185 ml (6 fl oz) milk
2 eggs
200 g (6½ oz) dried mixed fruit
80 g (2¾ oz) pecans, chopped
50 g (1¾ oz) hazelnuts, chopped
icing sugar, to dust

1 Preheat the oven to moderately hot 200°C (400°F/ Gas 6). Grease a 12-hole (125 ml/4 fl oz capacity) muffin tin with melted butter or oil. Sift the flours, baking powder, mixed spice, allspice and ginger into a large mixing bowl. Return the husks to the bowl.

2 Stir the butter, sugar and treacle in a small saucepan over low heat until the butter melts and the sugar dissolves. Remove from the heat. Whisk the milk and eggs together in a small jug.

3 Stir the mixed fruit, pecans and hazelnuts into the dry ingredients, and make a well in the centre. Pour the butter and egg mixtures into the well and stir with a metal spoon until just combined. Do not overmix—the mixture should be lumpy.

4 Spoon the mixture into the muffin tin, filling each hole about three-quarters full. Bake for 15–18 minutes, or until a skewer comes out clean when inserted into the centre of a muffin. Leave the muffins in the tin for 5 minutes before lifting out onto a wire rack to cool. Dust with sifted icing sugar before serving.

Chocolate and orange muffins

*A classic combination of flavours, these rich muffins have a dark creamy topping
made with chocolate and Cointreau, the sweet orange-flavoured liqueur.*

Preparation time 25 minutes
Total cooking time 25 minutes
Makes 12 medium muffins

150 g (5 oz) dark chocolate, chopped
75 g (2¹/₂ oz) unsalted butter, chopped
300 g (10 oz) self-raising flour
75 g (2¹/₂ oz) plain flour
3 tablespoons cocoa powder
3 tablespoons caster sugar
2 eggs
250 ml (8 fl oz) milk
1 tablespoon finely grated orange rind

TOPPING
200 g (6¹/₂ oz) dark chocolate, chopped
60 g (2 oz) unsalted butter, chopped
1 tablespoon Cointreau

shreds of orange rind, to decorate

1 Preheat the oven to hot 210°C (415°F/Gas 6–7).
Brush a 12-hole (125 ml/4 fl oz capacity) muffin tin
with melted butter or oil. Place the chocolate and butter
in a heatproof bowl standing over a pan of barely
simmering water. Stir occasionally, until the chocolate
and butter are melted. Remove from the heat.

2 Sift the flours and cocoa powder into a large mixing
bowl. Stir in the sugar and make a well in the centre.
Whisk the eggs, milk and orange rind together in a jug,
and pour into the well in the dry ingredients along with
the melted chocolate mixture. Stir with a metal spoon
until just combined. Do not overmix—the mixture
should be lumpy.

3 Spoon the mixture into the muffin tin, filling each
hole to about three-quarters full. Bake for 20 minutes,
or until a skewer comes out clean when inserted into
the centre of a muffin. Leave the muffins in the tin for
5 minutes, then lift out onto a wire rack to cool
completely before spreading with the topping.

4 To make the topping, place the chocolate and butter
in a heatproof bowl standing over a pan of barely
simmering water. Stir occasionally, until the chocolate
and butter are melted and combined. Remove from the
heat, stir in the Cointreau, and leave to cool until the
topping is thick enough to spread on top of the muffins.
Decorate with shreds of orange rind before serving.

Date and walnut muffins

These muffins are particularly suitable for lunch boxes, and can also be made as larger muffins. To do this, use a six-hole muffin tin and increase the baking time by approximately ten minutes.

*Preparation time **20 minutes***
*Total cooking time **25 minutes***
Makes 12 medium muffins

200 g (6¹/₂ oz) fresh or dried dates, pitted and chopped
100 g (3¹/₄ oz) unsalted butter
115 g (3³/₄ oz) soft brown sugar
225 g (7¹/₄ oz) self-raising flour
75 g (2¹/₂ oz) plain flour
125 g (4 oz) walnuts, toasted and chopped (see Chef's tip)
2 eggs, lightly beaten
icing sugar, to dust

1 Preheat the oven to hot 210°C (415°F/Gas 6–7). Brush a 12-hole (125 ml/4 fl oz capacity) muffin tin with melted butter or oil. Place 250 ml (8 fl oz) water in a pan with the dates, butter and sugar, and stir over low heat until the butter has melted. Bring to the boil, then remove from the heat and allow the mixture to cool to room temperature.

2 Sift the flours into a large mixing bowl, and stir in the walnuts. Make a well in the centre and pour in the date mixture along with the eggs, and stir with a metal spoon until the mixture is just combined. Do not overmix— the mixture should be lumpy.

3 Spoon the mixture into the muffin tin, filling each hole about three-quarters full. Bake for 20 minutes, or until a skewer comes out clean when inserted into the centre of a muffin. Leave the muffins in the tin for 5 minutes before lifting out onto a wire rack to cool. Dust with sifted icing sugar before serving.

Chef's tip To toast the nuts, spread them on a baking tray and bake in a moderate 180°C (350°F/Gas 4) oven for 5–7 minutes, or until lightly browned.

Muesli muffins

There are a number of ways of eating muesli—with fruit, yoghurt, milk or, as in this case, as part of a muffin. These muffins are ideal served at breakfast, and are also good served with a warm fruit compote.

Preparation time **15 minutes**
Total cooking time **20 minutes**
Makes 12 medium muffins

150 g (5 oz) self-raising flour
75 g (2¹/2 oz) wholemeal self-raising flour
100 g (3¹/4 oz) toasted muesli
115 g (3³/4 oz) soft brown sugar
85 g (2³/4 oz) raisins
250 ml (8 fl oz) milk
2 eggs
100 g (3¹/4 oz) unsalted butter,
melted
75 g (2¹/2 oz) toasted muesli,
extra

1 Preheat the oven to hot 210°C (415°F/Gas 6–7). Brush a 12-hole (125 ml/4 fl oz capacity) muffin tin with melted butter or oil. Sift the flours together and return the husks to the bowl. Stir in the muesli, sugar and raisins, and make a well in the centre.

2 Whisk the milk and eggs together, and add to the well in the dry ingredients along with the butter. Stir with a metal spoon until just combined. Do not overmix—the mixture should be lumpy.

3 Spoon the mixture into the muffin tin, filling each hole about three-quarters full. Sprinkle the extra muesli on top of the unbaked muffins and press on gently. Bake for 20 minutes, or until a skewer comes out clean when inserted into the centre of a muffin. Leave the muffins in the tin for 5 minutes before lifting out onto a wire rack to cool. Delicious served warm with butter.

Passion fruit and yoghurt muffins

The sweet tang and crunch of the passion fruit seeds, and the melt-in-the-mouth frosting,
will make these muffins appeal to all ages.

Preparation time *30 minutes*
Total cooking time *30 minutes*
Makes 12 medium muffins

300 g (10 oz) self-raising flour
75 g (2¹/₂ oz) plain flour
4 tablespoons caster sugar
125 g (4 oz) unsalted butter
3 tablespoons honey
2 eggs, lightly beaten
250 g (8 oz) plain yoghurt
125 g (4 oz) passion fruit pulp (see Chef's tip)

PASSION FRUIT FROSTING
100 g (3¹/₄ oz) unsalted butter, softened
125 g (4 oz) icing sugar
2 tablespoons passion fruit pulp (see Chef's tip)

1 Preheat the oven to hot 210°C (415°F/Gas 6–7). Brush a 12-hole (125 ml/4 fl oz capacity) muffin tin with melted butter or oil. Sift the flours into a large mixing bowl, stir in the sugar and make a well in the centre.

2 Place the butter and honey in a small pan, and stir over low heat until melted and blended. Remove from the heat, cool slightly, then pour into the well in the dry ingredients along with the eggs, yoghurt and passion fruit pulp. Stir with a metal spoon until the mixture is just combined. Do not overmix—the mixture should be lumpy.

3 Spoon the mixture into the muffin tin, filling each hole about three-quarters full. Bake for 20–25 minutes, or until a skewer comes out clean when inserted into the centre of a muffin. Leave the muffins in the tin for 5 minutes, then lift out onto a wire rack to cool completely before spreading with the frosting.

4 To make the passion fruit frosting, beat the butter and icing sugar with electric beaters until light and creamy. Beat in the passion fruit pulp until well mixed, then spread onto the muffins.

Chef's tip You will need about six large passion fruit for this recipe.

Raspberry streusel muffins

The much-loved streusel topping is used in this recipe for raspberry streusel muffins. Any type of berry could be substituted for raspberries to give perfect results every time.

*Preparation time **25 minutes***
*Total cooking time **20 minutes***
Makes 12 medium muffins

225 g (7¼ oz) self-raising flour
150 g (5 oz) plain flour
115 g (3¾ oz) soft brown sugar
150 g (5 oz) fresh or frozen raspberries
  (see Chef's tips)
2 eggs
250 ml (8 fl oz) milk
125 g (4 oz) unsalted butter, melted

STREUSEL TOPPING
50 g (1¾ oz) plain flour
30 g (1 oz) unsalted butter, chilled and cubed
2 tablespoons soft brown sugar

1 Preheat the oven to hot 210°C (415°F/Gas 6–7). Brush a 12-hole (125 ml/4 fl oz capacity) muffin tin with melted butter or oil. Sift the self-raising and plain flour into a large mixing bowl, stir in the brown sugar and raspberries, and make a well in the centre.

2 Whisk the eggs and milk together in a jug, and pour into the well in the dry ingredients along with the butter. Stir with a metal spoon until just combined. Do not overmix—the mixture should be lumpy. Spoon the mixture into the muffin tin, filling each hole about three-quarters full.

3 To make the topping, place the flour, butter and sugar in a small bowl, and rub together with your fingertips until crumbly. Sprinkle on top of the unbaked muffins, and press on gently.

4 Bake for 20 minutes, or until a skewer comes out clean when inserted into the centre of a muffin. Leave the muffins in the tin for 5 minutes before lifting out onto a wire rack to cool.

Chef's tips Different types of berries, such as blackberries, boysenberries or mulberries, can be used instead of the raspberries. Large berries, such as strawberries, should be chopped into smaller pieces.

If using frozen raspberries, use them straight from the freezer. Do not allow them to thaw, or they will discolour the muffin mixture.

Pumpkin muffins

The delicate flavour of spices, and the mild, sweet flesh of the pumpkin are a perfect combination.
These muffins are ideal for picnics, breakfast or mid-morning snacks.

Preparation time **15 minutes**
Total cooking time **40 minutes**
Makes 12 medium muffins

500 g (1 lb) peeled and cubed
  pumpkin
100 g (3¼ oz) wholemeal self-raising flour
200 g (6½ oz) self-raising flour
75 g (2½ oz) plain flour
½ teaspoon mixed spice
¼ teaspoon ground nutmeg
115 g (3¾ oz) soft brown sugar
2 eggs
125 ml (4 fl oz) vegetable oil
125 ml (4 fl oz) milk
1 teaspoon vanilla extract or essence

1 Preheat the oven to hot 210°C (415°F/Gas 6–7). Brush a 12-hole (125 ml/4 fl oz capacity) muffin tin with melted butter or oil. Steam or microwave the pumpkin until tender, then drain well and mash. Leave to cool.

2 Sift the flours, mixed spice and nutmeg into a large mixing bowl, returning the husks to the bowl. Stir in the sugar and make a well in the centre.

3 Whisk the eggs, oil, milk and vanilla together, and pour into the well in the dry ingredients with the pumpkin. Stir with a metal spoon until just combined. Do not overmix—the mixture should be lumpy.

4 Spoon the mixture into the muffin tin, filling each hole about three-quarters full. Bake for 20–25 minutes, or until a skewer comes out clean when inserted into the centre of a muffin. Leave the muffins in the tin for 5 minutes before lifting out onto a wire rack to cool.

Corn muffins

Cornmeal, which resembles a coarse polenta, is made from ground corn kernels.
It is used here with whole corn kernels to produce these bright savoury muffins.

Preparation time **15 minutes**
Total cooking time **20 minutes**
Makes 12 medium muffins

225 g (7 1/4 oz) self-raising flour
pinch of cayenne pepper
150 g (5 oz) cornmeal
60 g (2 oz) Cheddar, finely grated
310 g (10 oz) can of corn kernels, drained
   (see Chef's tip)
250 ml (8 fl oz) milk
2 eggs
100 g (3 1/4 oz) unsalted butter, melted

1 Preheat the oven to hot 210°C (415°F/Gas 6–7). Brush a 12-hole (125 ml/4 fl oz capacity) muffin tin with melted butter or oil. Sift the flour and cayenne pepper into a large bowl. Stir in the cornmeal, cheese and corn kernels, and make a well in the centre.

2 Whisk the milk and eggs together in a jug, and pour into the well in the dry ingredients along with the butter. Stir with a metal spoon until just combined. Do not overmix—the mixture should be lumpy. Spoon the mixture into the muffin tin, filling each hole about three-quarters full.

3 Bake for 20 minutes, or until a skewer comes out clean when inserted into the centre of a muffin. Leave the muffins in the tin for 5 minutes before lifting out onto a wire rack to cool.

Chef's tip You can also use 240 g (7 1/2 oz) fresh or frozen corn kernels. Cook them in boiling water until they are tender, then drain and cool before using.

Seeded cheese muffins

These savoury muffins are so simple to prepare, and make a delicious change from the French stick for a 'ploughman's lunch'. Alternatively, serve with pickles for a quick snack.

*Preparation time **20 minutes***
*Total cooking time **25 minutes***
Makes 12 medium muffins

4 tablespoons sesame seeds
4 tablespoons sunflower seeds
50 g (1³/4 oz) pumpkin seeds (pepitas)
300 g (10 oz) self-raising flour
75 g (2¹/2 oz) plain flour
pinch of salt
60 g (2 oz) Cheddar, grated
50 g (1³/4 oz) Parmesan, grated
2 eggs
250 ml (8 fl oz) milk
125 g (4 oz) unsalted butter,
  melted
1 tablespoon sesame seeds, extra

1 Preheat the oven to hot 210°C (415°F/Gas 6–7). Brush a 12-hole (125 ml/4 fl oz capacity) muffin tin with melted butter or oil. Place the sesame, sunflower and pumpkin seeds in a frying pan, and dry-fry over low heat for a few minutes, or until the sesame seeds are golden. Transfer to a large mixing bowl to cool. Sift the flours and salt onto the seeds, stir in the cheeses, and make a well in the centre.

2 Whisk the eggs and milk together in a jug, and add to the well in the dry ingredients along with the butter. Stir with a metal spoon until just combined. Do not overmix—the mixture should be lumpy. Spoon into the muffin tin, filling each hole about three-quarters full. Sprinkle with the extra sesame seeds.

3 Bake for 20 minutes, or until a skewer comes out clean when inserted into the centre of a muffin. Leave the muffins in the tin for 5 minutes before lifting out onto a wire rack to cool.

Cheese and herb muffins

Cheese and herb muffins are an excellent accompaniment to soups and stews.
They are also delicious spread with butter.

Preparation time **25 minutes**
Total cooking time **20 minutes**
Makes 12 medium muffins

225 g (7 1/4 oz) self-raising flour
155 g (5 oz) wholemeal self-raising flour
pinch of cayenne pepper
pinch of salt
2 tablespoons finely chopped fresh parsley
2 tablespoons finely chopped fresh chives
2 tablespoons fresh thyme leaves
125 g (4 oz) Cheddar, grated
2 eggs
250 ml (8 fl oz) milk
125 g (4 oz) unsalted butter, melted

1 Preheat the oven to hot 210°C (415°F/Gas 6–7). Brush a 12-hole (125 ml/4 fl oz capacity) muffin tin with melted butter or oil. Sift the flours, cayenne pepper and salt into a large bowl, and return the husks to the bowl. Stir in the herbs and cheese, and make a well in the centre.

2 Whisk the eggs and milk together in a jug, and pour into the well in the dry ingredients along with the butter. Stir with a metal spoon until just combined. Do not overmix—the mixture should be lumpy.

3 Spoon the mixture into the muffin tin, filling each hole about three-quarters full. Bake for 20 minutes, or until a skewer comes out clean when inserted into the centre of a muffin. Leave the muffins in the tin for 5 minutes before lifting out onto a wire rack to cool.

Bacon muffins

Bacon muffins are perfect for a leisurely weekend brunch with scrambled or poached eggs, or simply with butter. When making these muffins, it is very important not to overmix the batter or the muffins will be tough and rubbery.

*Preparation time **25 minutes***
*Total cooking time **30 minutes***
Makes 12 medium muffins

2 teaspoons oil
6 rashers bacon, finely chopped
1 large onion, finely chopped
300 g (10 oz) self-raising flour
75 g (2¹/2 oz) plain flour
pinch of salt
1 tablespoon chopped fresh parsley
2 eggs
250 ml (8 fl oz) milk
125 g (4 oz) unsalted butter, melted

1 Preheat the oven to hot 210°C (415°F/Gas 6–7). Brush a 12-hole (125 ml/4 fl oz capacity) muffin tin with melted butter or oil. Heat the oil in a frying pan and cook the bacon until it is brown and crisp. Remove from the pan and drain on crumpled paper towels. Cook the onion in the same pan until it is very soft and lightly golden, then leave to cool.

2 Sift the flours and salt into a large bowl, stir in the parsley, and make a well in the centre. Whisk the eggs and milk together in a jug, and pour into the well in the dry ingredients. Add the melted butter, cooled bacon and onion, and stir with a metal spoon until just combined. Do not overmix—the mixture should be lumpy.

3 Spoon the mixture into the muffin tin, filling each hole to about three-quarters full. Bake for 20 minutes, or until a skewer comes out clean when inserted into the centre of a muffin. Leave the muffins in the tin for 5 minutes before lifting out onto a wire rack to cool.

Olive, rosemary and Parmesan muffins

The delicious combination of complementary flavours in these muffins makes them the ideal accompaniment to a crisp green salad on a hot summer's day.

Preparation time **25 minutes**
Total cooking time **20 minutes**
Makes 12 medium muffins

300 g (10 oz) self-raising flour
75 g (2¹/2 oz) plain flour
pinch of salt
**175 g (5³/4 oz) black olives, pitted
  and chopped**
35 g (1¹/4 oz) Parmesan, finely grated
1 tablespoon finely chopped fresh rosemary
2 eggs
250 ml (8 fl oz) milk
125 g (4 oz) unsalted butter, melted

1 Preheat the oven to hot 210°C (415°F/Gas 6–7). Brush a 12-hole (125 ml/4 fl oz capacity) muffin tin with melted butter or oil. Sift the flours and salt into a large bowl, stir in the olives, Parmesan and rosemary, and make a well in the centre.

2 Whisk the eggs and milk together in a jug, and pour into the well in the dry ingredients along with the butter. Stir with a metal spoon until just combined. Do not overmix—the mixture should be lumpy. Spoon the mixture into the muffin tin, filling each hole about three-quarters full.

3 Bake for 20 minutes, or until a skewer comes out clean when inserted into the centre of a muffin. Leave in the tin for 5 minutes before lifting out onto a wire rack to cool.

Red capsicum and feta muffins

*These muffins are best eaten on the day they are made. If this is impractical, however,
simply reheat in a moderate oven for a few minutes before serving.*

Preparation time 30 minutes
Total cooking time 30 minutes
Makes 12 medium muffins

1 large red capsicum (pepper)
300 g (10 oz) self-raising flour
75 g (2¹/2 oz) plain flour
pinch of salt
150 g (5 oz) feta cheese, crumbled
2 eggs
250 ml (8 fl oz) milk
125 g (4 oz) unsalted butter, melted

1 Preheat the oven to hot 210°C (415°F/Gas 6–7). Brush a 12-hole (125 ml/4 fl oz capacity) muffin tin with melted butter or oil. Remove the seeds and membrane from the capsicum, and cut it into large flattish pieces. Roast under a hot grill until the skin blackens and blisters, then transfer to a plastic bag to cool. Peel away and discard the skin, and chop the flesh.

2 Sift the flours and salt into a large bowl, stir in the capsicum and feta, and make a well in the centre.

3 Whisk the eggs and milk together in a jug, and pour into the well in the dry ingredients along with the butter. Stir with a metal spoon until just combined. Do not overmix—the mixture should be lumpy.

4 Spoon the mixture into the muffin tin, filling each hole about three-quarters full. Bake for 20 minutes, or until a skewer comes out clean when inserted into the centre of a muffin. Leave the muffins in the tin for 5 minutes before lifting out onto a wire rack to cool.

Ham and cheese muffins

Delicious served warm with a vegetable soup or tomato salad, these muffins can also be made with smoked ham, Gruyère cheese or a tablespoon of chopped fresh herbs.

*Preparation time **20 minutes***
*Total cooking time **25 minutes***
Makes 12 medium muffins

3 spring onions, finely chopped
1 teaspoon oil
300 g (10 oz) self-raising flour
75 g (2¹/₂ oz) plain flour
pinch of salt
pinch of dry mustard powder
175 g (5³/₄ oz) ham, chopped
125 g (4 oz) Cheddar, grated
2 eggs
250 ml (8 fl oz) milk
125 g (4 oz) unsalted butter, melted

1 Preheat the oven to hot 210°C (415°F/Gas 6–7). Brush a 12-hole (125 ml/4 fl oz capacity) muffin tin with melted butter or oil. Fry the spring onions in the oil for 2–3 minutes, or until soft. Sift the flours, salt and mustard powder into a large bowl, and season well with freshly ground black pepper. Stir in the ham, cheese and spring onion, and make a well in the centre.

2 Whisk the eggs and milk together in a jug, and add to the well in the dry ingredients along with the butter. Stir with a metal spoon until just combined. Do not overmix—the mixture should be lumpy.

3 Spoon the mixture into the muffin tin, filling each hole about three-quarters full. Bake for 20 minutes, or until a skewer comes out clean when inserted into the centre of a muffin. Leave the muffins in the tin for 5 minutes before lifting out onto a wire rack to cool.

Chef's techniques

◆

Preparing and filling the tin

If a recipe makes 6 large muffins, you can use a 12-hole tin and make 12 medium muffins.

Lightly brush each hole of the muffin tin with melted butter or oil, or spray with non-stick cooking oil.

Alternatively, place a paper muffin case in each hole of the muffin tin.

Gently spoon the muffin mixture into the prepared tin, using another spoon to scrape the mixture off.

Melt-and-mix method

This is the most common method used to prepare muffins, resulting in a light, moist texture.

Sift the flours into a large mixing bowl, stir in the sugar and remaining dry ingredients. Make a well in the centre.

Melt the butter in a small saucepan, then remove from the heat and allow to cool slightly.

Combine the eggs and milk in a jug, then pour into the well in the dry ingredients along with the cooled butter.

Using a large metal spoon, incorporate the wet and dry mixtures with a folding motion. Stir until just combined, but do not overmix—the batter should be lumpy—otherwise the muffins will be tough and rubbery.

Testing for doneness

Bake the muffins as directed in the recipe, then test if they are cooked using either of these methods.

If a skewer comes out clean when inserted into the centre of a muffin, the muffins are cooked.

If a muffin springs back when lightly pressed with your fingertips, the muffins are cooked.

Removing from the tin

Most muffins should be left for 5 minutes to set before they are removed from the tin.

Gently loosen the edges of the muffins with a palette knife.

Carefully lift the muffins from the tin and place on a wire rack to cool.

Streusel topping

Streusel toppings add a lovely crunchy texture to muffins.

Sprinkle the streusel topping evenly over the top of the unbaked muffin mixture.

Freezing muffins

Muffins will freeze well for up to a month. You can wrap them individually, and enjoy one at a time.

Place the muffins in a freezer bag and remove as much air as possible. Seal well, and freeze. When ready to use, thaw at room temperature or wrap in foil and heat in a moderate 180°C (350°F/Gas 4) oven.

Published by Murdoch Books® a division of Murdoch Magazines Pty Limited, 45 Jones Street, Ultimo NSW 2007.

Murdoch Books and Le Cordon Bleu thank the 32 masterchefs of all the Le Cordon Bleu Schools, whose knowledge and expertise have made this book possible, especially: Chef Cliche (MOF), Chef Terrien, Chef Boucheret, Chef Duchêne (MOF), Chef Guillut, Chef Steneck, Paris; Chef Males, Chef Walsh, Chef Hardy, London; Chef Chantefort, Chef Bertin, Chef Jambert, Chef Honda, Tokyo; Chef Salembien, Chef Boutin, Chef Harris, Sydney; Chef Lawes, Adelaide; Chef Guiet, Chef Denis, Ottawa. Of the many students who helped the Chefs test each recipe, a special mention to graduates David Welch and Allen Wertheim. A very special acknowledgment to Directors Susan Eckstein, Great Britain, and Kathy Shaw, Paris, who have been responsible for the coordination of the Le Cordon Bleu team throughout this series.

Murdoch Books®
Managing Editor: Kay Halsey
Series Concept, Design and Art Direction: Juliet Cohen
Editors: Elizabeth Cotton, Justine Upex
Food Director: Jody Vassallo
Food Editors: Kathy Knudsen, Dimitra Stais, Tracy Rutherford
Designer: Michèle Lichtenberger
Photographer: Andre Martin
Food Stylist: Mary Harris
Food Preparation: Tracy Rutherford
Chef's Techniques Photographer: Reg Morrison
Home Economists: Michelle Lawton, Kerrie Mullins, Kerrie Ray

CEO & Publisher: Anne Wilson
Publishing Director: Catie Ziller
General Manager: Mark Smith
Creative Director: Marylouise Brammer
International Sales Director: Mark Newman

National Library of Australia Cataloguing-in-Publication Data
Muffins. ISBN 0 86411 748 5. 1. Muffins. (Series: Le Cordon Bleu home collection). 641.815

Printed by Toppan Printing (S) Pte Ltd
First Printed 1998
©Design and photography Murdoch Books® 1998
©Text Le Cordon Bleu 1998
Distributed in the UK by D Services, 6 Euston Street, Freemen's Common, Leicester LE2 7SS Tel 0116-254-7671 Fax 0116-254-4670. Distributed in Canada by Whitecap (Vancouver) Ltd, 351 Lynn Avenue, North Vancouver, BC V7J 2C4 Tel 604-980-9852 Fax 604-980-8197 or Whitecap (Ontario) Ltd, 47 Coldwater Road, North York, ON M3B 1Y8 Tel 416-444-3442 Fax 416-444-6630

The Publisher and Le Cordon Bleu wish to thank Carole Sweetnam for her help with this series.
Front cover: Blueberry muffins (shown with whipped cream and fresh blueberries).

IMPORTANT INFORMATION

CONVERSION GUIDE

1 cup = 250 ml (8 fl oz)
1 Australian tablespoon = 20 ml (4 teaspoons)
1 UK tablespoon = 15 ml (3 teaspoons)

NOTE: We have used 20 ml tablespoons. If you are using a 15 ml tablespoon, for most recipes the difference will be negligible. For recipes using baking powder, gelatine, bicarbonate of soda and flour, add an extra teaspoon for each tablespoon specified.

CUP CONVERSIONS—DRY INGREDIENTS

1 cup flour, plain or self-raising = 125 g (4 oz)
1 cup sugar, caster = 250 g (8 oz)
1 cup breadcrumbs, dry = 125 g (4 oz)

IMPORTANT: Those who might be at risk from the effects of salmonella food poisoning (the elderly, pregnant women, young children and those suffering from immune deficiency diseases) should consult their GP with any concerns about eating raw eggs.